A CONTRIBUTION TO TONGAN SOMATOLOGY

By Louis R. Sullivan

BASED ON THE FIELD STUDIES OF E. W. GIFFORD AND W. C. MCKERN

Memoirs of the Bernice Pauahi Bishop Museum
Volume VIII—Number 4

WITH PLATES XXXVI-XXXIX

BAYARD DOMINICK EXPEDITION

Publication Number 2

HONOLULU, HAWAII
BISHOP MUSEUM PRESS
1922

A CONTRIBUTION TO TONGAN SOMATOLOGY

By LOUIS R. SULLIVAN

Based on the field studies of E. W. Gifford and W. C. McKern

INTRODUCTION

THE somatological studies in Tonga followed the plan previously used for Samoa.[1] The field records were made by E. W. Gifford and W. C. McKern, assisted by Delila S. Gifford and show evidence of unusual care and discrimination; the mathematical computations were prepared by my wife, Bessie P. Sullivan. By arrangement between the American Museum of Natural History and the Bishop Museum the analysis of the data and the preparation of the results for publication constitute my share of the work.

Mr. Gifford and Mr. McKern call attention to the assistance rendered by many individuals in Tonga and especially to the kindness shown by Their Majesties Queen Charlotte Tupou and Prince Consort William Tungi, who permitted themselves to be measured, thus graciously setting an example that was gladly followed by their loyal subjects. The Privy Council also greatly aided the expedition by instructing the Minister of Police, Mr. Job Koho, to provide the required number of persons for each day's examinations.

The material on which this paper is based consists of complete descriptions and measurements of 225 persons, 121 men and 104 women. Of these 10 were of mixed racial descent and their records were therefore discarded. Of the remaining 215, 184 were adults more than twenty years of age and 31 adolescents. The averages of non-quantitative descriptions are based on observations of young and old from the age of sixteen upward; the averages of all measurements except stature are based on measurements of persons of both sexes eighteen years old and upward.

By nativity the individuals examined are distributed as follows: Niuatoputapu 4; Niuafoou 1; Vavau group 25; Haapai group 40 (in detail, Haano 8, Nomuka 2, Uiha 4, Lifuka 6, other places 20); Tongatabu 148 (Nukualofa 47, other places 101); Eua 5; elsewhere 2. The material was not consciously selected and represents persons of all social classes and occupations. It may be regarded as a fair qualitative sample of the Tongan people.

---

[1] Sullivan, L. A., A contribution to Samoan somatology: B. P. Bishop Mus. Mem. vol. viii, No. 2, 1921.

According to the Tongan census of 1920 there were at that time 23,128 Tongans in the group. Census returns for the past twenty years show that as a whole the Tongan population is increasing slowly. A temporary decrease was shown in the reports for 1918 and 1919, but returns for 1920 show a slight increase. It is of interest to notice also that there has been considerably less modern mixture with other races than in many other Polynesian groups. The census of 1917 records only 300 mixed bloods. How accurate this may be I do not know, but since the same census records only 347 Europeans and 529 other Pacific islanders, it is apparent that there have been fewer opportunities and temptations to marry outside the race than there have been in many other places where the aboriginal inhabitants are greatly outnumbered by the Europeans or Orientals. These facts should be borne in mind.

METHOD

All measurements were taken in accordance with the regulations of the International Agreement. The technique is described in some detail in my previous paper[2] but for the sake of convenience is here repeated in outline. Each measurement and index is numbered, and in the tables throughout this paper these numbers refer consistently to the same measurements.

ANTHROPOMETRIC CHARACTERS

1. Stature: recorded to the nearest centimeter (shoes removed).
2. Maximum head length: from the glabella to the opisthocranium.
3. Maximum head width.
4. Minimum frontal diameter: transverse.
5. Maximum face width or bizygomatic diameter.
6. Bigonial diameter at the angle of the mandible avoiding as much of the muscles as possible.
7. Anatomical face height; nasion to gnathion.
8. Nose height nasion to subnasale.
9. Nasal width; alare to alare.
10. Physiognomic ear length or height.
11. Physiognomic ear breadth.

INDICES

12. Cephalic or length-breadth index $= \dfrac{\text{measurement No. } 3 \times 100}{\text{measurement No. } 2}$

13. Transverse fronto-parietal index $= \dfrac{\text{measurement No. } 4 \times 100}{\text{measurement No. } 3}$

14. Transverse cephalo-facial index $= \dfrac{\text{measurement No. } 5 \times 100}{\text{measurement No. } 3}$

15. Zygomatico-frontal index $= \dfrac{\text{measurement No. } 4 \times 100}{\text{measurement No. } 5}$
    (Sometimes designated as the jugo-frontal index)

16. Zygomatico-mandibular index $= \dfrac{\text{measurement No. } 6 \times 100}{\text{measurement No. } 5}$
    (Sometimes designated as the jugo-mandibular index)

17. Anatomical facial index $= \dfrac{\text{measurement No. } 7 \times 100}{\text{measurement No. } 5}$

18. Nasal index $= \dfrac{\text{measurement No. } 9 \times 100}{\text{measurement No. } 8}$

19. Physiognomic ear index $= \dfrac{\text{measurement No. } 11 \times 100}{\text{measurement No. } 10}$

The anthropometric data were supplemented by observations on characters not quantitatively measurable. In view of the widespread misconception as to the nature of these characters and their value in somatology, it seems desirable to

[2] Op. cit.

236 *Memoirs Bernice P. Bishop Museum*

point out in some detail just what has been attempted in describing characters that do not lend themselves readily to measurement. The fact that anthropologists have carelessly spoken of "types" of hair form, hair color, or eye color has given the erroneous impression—not only to the general reader but to many anthropologists as well—that these types actually exist in nature and that it is possible, for example, to arrange all human eyes in four, five, or six color groups. Although it is universally recognized that all characters that lend themselves to actual measurement show a continuous variation with a tendency for a large percentage of the individuals measured to cluster around a median or mean point, yet it is difficult to dislodge the idea that other characters such as color or form, which cannot be accurately measured with existing apparatus, have a discontinuous distribution. The body height or stature of the Scots, for example, ranges from 158 centimeters to 186 centimeters and averages about 172 centimeters. Very few Scotchmen are as short as 158 centimeters and very few are as tall as 186 centimeters. In progressing from the extremes towards the mean the number of individuals at each step increases. It is apparent to anyone who has endeavored to classify characters which do not lend themselves to measurement that in them he is dealing with exactly the same type of continuous variation. When the metric rod cannot be applied, standards are set up along the range of variation, separated widely enough to permit of distinguishing each from the standard preceding or following it, and an endeavor is made to classify the material on this basis. The attempt to classify all existing forms of hair as straight, low waves, deep waves, curly, frizzly, or woolly, produces results very similar to those which might be expected if the stature of all men were measured with a rod graduated in 10 centimeter intervals from 130 to 190 centimeters. A man's stature would be recorded as 130, 140, 150, 160, 170, 180, or 190 centimeters; yet it is obvious that the stature of many men would actually be 135, 136, or 137 centimeters. The rod is not graduated finely enough to record the true distribution of the measurements. In a sense hair classes may be compared with these 10-centimeter intervals. For example, straight hair might well correspond with the 130-centimeter mark and woolly hair with the 190-centimeter mark or vice versa. But at this point the analogy breaks down. It is not certain that low waves, deep waves, and other hair forms correspond exactly to the 140- and 150-centimeter points. Roughly they probably do. But by far the greatest difference in the two methods and one that should always be kept in mind in the analysis of data is that in the classification of these descriptive or attribute characters, so called, the "metric rod" exists only in the mind of the observer and is by no means a uniform or universal standard. This lack of a fixed standard makes difficult not only the comparison of small differences found by different observers, but also to a lesser extent those found at different times by the same observer. As the standard is purely visual, constructed largely upon the expe-

[6]

riences of each observer, it necessarily fluctuates constantly, varying with new experiences.

Despite the varying standards many of these non-measurable characters have proved to be of such great value in pointing out racial similarities and differences that no general somatological study is justified in omitting them. In pointing out the sources of error in data of this sort it is not my purpose to belittle their value or to imply that the size of the error is uniform for all characters. Although two observers might disagree as to whether a given sample of hair were low-waved, or straight, yet they would be much less likely to disagree as to whether it were straight or deeply waved, and still less likely to disagree as to whether it were straight or curly. The same considerations apply to color.

Recognizing then the fact of the continuous variation in these characters, I have described them as if they were discontinuous. For purposes of this paper hair form is classified as straight, low-waved, deep-waved, curly, frizzly, and woolly, and the color is designated as black, dark brown, reddish-brown, light brown, blond, golden, red, and gray. The amount of beard on the upper cheek, lower cheek, and chin and the amount of body hair on the chest, forearm, and leg was described as none, slight, medium, and heavy. Eye color is classified as black, dark brown, and light brown, blue, gray, blue-brown, and gray-brown. The amount of conjunctival pigment is classified roughly in accordance with the appearance of the sclera—white and clear, muddy, speckled, or mottled. The development or lack of development of the epicanthic (Mongoloid) eye fold is described as absent, slight, medium, or marked. The elevation of the nasal bridge has been

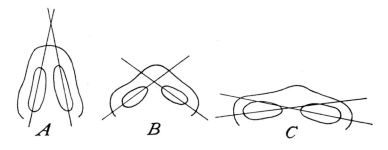

FIGURE 1. Diagram illustrating terminology used to describe the form of the nostrils: *A*, antero-posterior nostrils; *B*, obliquely placed nostrils; *C*, transverse nostrils.

estimated in terms of low, medium, or high. The form and direction of the nostrils are roughly classed, according to the direction of the long axis of each nostril, as antero-posterior, oblique, or transverse. (See figs. 1 and 2.) The slope of the forehead is estimated as vertical, moderate slope, or low. The development of the glabella is indicated by the terms smooth, medium, and prominent. The thickness

238　　　　　　*Memoirs Bernice P. Bishop Museum*

of the lips is recorded as thin, medium, or thick. Prognathism, which in a living person is a complex and somewhat elusive character, is described as absent, slight, medium, or marked. In the ears the development of the lobes (small or large, attached or separate), the roll of the helix (rolled one-third, two-thirds, three-thirds, or flat), and the presence or absence of Darwin's tubercle were recorded.

Particular care was taken to record the form of the upper incisor teeth with a view to determining the presence or absence of the shovel-shaped incisors. Although primarily described by Hrdlicka[3] as shovel-shaped this condition of the incisor and other teeth has more recently been described by the same author as keilodonty and koilomorphy. As the fossa is dependent on the formation of the rim, it will be sufficiently clear and less cumbersome to discuss this condition in terms of rim development or keilodonty. In this paper classes of no rim, trace of rim, medium rim, and marked rim correspond to Hrdlicka's classes of no shovel, plain trace, semi-shovel, shovel-shaped. The condition is well described by Hrdlicka:[4] "The lingual surface of the well developed shovel-shaped incisor is very striking. The usual moderate concavity from above downward is replaced by a triangular to rounded or oblong deep fossa. The base of the fossa is formed by the free edge of the tooth, its summit reaches upwards near to the gum. The fossa is bounded laterally and generally also distally, hence on all sides by a stout rim of enamel."

DESCRIPTION OF THE TONGANS

The results of the seriation and averages are summarized in Tables I, II, and III. In Table I we find a fairly normal distribution in all anthropometric characters. The number of persons concerned in each character is so small that any departure from the normal cannot be regarded too seriously. Doubling the class interval is usually sufficient to smooth the curve. Even after doing this, however, the distribution of head length and face width present a somewhat skewed distribution. Indications of bimodality are also noticeable in the bigonial diameter, face height, and face index distribution. At present the significance or non-significance of these facts is not clear.

---

[3] Hrdlicka, Ales, Shovel-shaped teeth: Am. Jour. of Phys. Anthr., vol. III, p. 429, 1920.
[4] Op. cit., p. 429.

Sullivan—Tongan Somatology

TABLE I.—SERIATION OF ANTHROPOMETRIC CHARACTERS IN ABSOLUTE NUMBERS

1. STATURE			2. HEAD LENGTH			3. HEAD WIDTH			4. MINIMUM FRONTAL		
Centimeters	Male	Female	Millimeters	Male	Female	Millimeters	Male	Female	Millimeters	Male	Female
150	......	1	170	......	2	140	......	1	90	......	....
1	......	0	1	......	0	1	......	1	1	......	....
2	......	1	2	......	1	2	......	2	2	1	....
3	......	1	3	1	2	3	......	2	3	0	1
4	......	4	4	0	1	4	......	6	4	2	1
5	......	2	5	0	1	5	1	7	5	1	3
6	......	1	6	1	2	6	2	9	6	2	0
7	......	5	7	0	6	7	2	7	7	2	4
8	......	4	8	0	4	8	5	5	8	1	5
9	......	6	9	0	5	9	3	9	9	3	11
160	1	7	180	0	6	150	6	8	100	8	7
1	1	7	1	2	5	1	6	8	1	4	7
2	0	7	2	9	4	2	6	4	2	10	7
3	0	6	3	4	12	3	10	2	3	11	7
4	1	4	4	5	4	4	13	6	4	14	7
5	5	5	5	2	2	5	12	9	5	14	10
6	3	4	6	9	4	6	15	0	6	8	5
7	5	3	7	5	9	7	7	3	7	5	5
8	1	2	8	4	3	8	8	2	8	6	4
9	5	6	9	7	5	9	6	1	9	3	4
170	9	1	190	10	2	160	5	0	110	7	1
1	3	3	1	9	4	1	2	2	11	4	2
2	7	2	2	5	0	2	4	1	12	2	1
3	6	2	3	7	4	3	1	1	13	1	0
4	10	1	4	5	1	4	1	0	14	2	4
5	4	0	5	4	4	5	0	1	15	3	....
6	8	0	6	3	1	6	0	....	16	1	....
7	8	0	7	4	1	7	2	....	17	0	....
8	3	0	8	2	1	8	......	....	18	0	....
9	3	0	9	7	0	9	......	....	19	1	....
180	2	0	200	1	0	170	......	....	Total	116	96
1	4	0	1	2	1	1	......	....			
2	1	1	2	2	....	2	......	....			
3	1	....	3	0	....	3	......	....			
4	0	....	4	4	....	4	......	....			
5	0	....	5	1	....	Total	117	97			
6	0	....	6	0	....						
7	0	....	7	0	....						
8	1	....	8	0	....						
9	0	....	9	0	....						
Total	92	88	210	1	....						
			11	0	....						
			12	0	....						
			13	1	....						
			14	......	....						
			Total	117	97						

240 Memoirs Bernice P. Bishop Museum

5. FACE WIDTH			6. BIGONIAL			7. FACE HEIGHT			8. NOSE HEIGHT		
Millimeters	Male	Female	Millimeters	Male	Female	Millimeters	Male	Female	Millimeters	Male	Female
120	......	....	90	......	3	100	......	....	40	......	....
1	......	....	1	......	2	1	......	....	1	......	....
2	......	1	2	1	3	2	......	....	2	......	....
3	......	0	3	1	4	3	......	....	3	......	....
4	......	1	4	2	2	4	......	1	4	......	....
5	......	0	5	4	3	5	......	0	5	......	....
6	......	1	6	2	10	6	......	0	6	......	....
7	......	1	7	1	11	7	......	0	7	1	....
8	......	2	8	2	3	8	......	0	8	2	....
9	......	1	9	6	7	9	......	0	9	0	3
130	......	6	100	9	14	110	......	0	50	2	2
1	2	5	1	7	7	11	......	0	1	0	2
2	2	4	2	10	5	12	2	0	2	5	6
3	4	6	3	8	4	13	0	0	3	5	6
4	0	6	4	9	4	14	0	2	4	7	7
5	3	5	5	4	3	15	1	1	5	15	9
6	1	6	6	5	5	16	0	3	6	15	15
7	1	10	7	4	4	17	1	5	7	13	9
8	7	10	8	9	0	18	3	2	8	6	7
9	8	3	9	5	0	19	6	11	9	7	7
140	8	3	110	5	0	120	6	5	60	11	10
1	9	6	11	8	1	1	7	0	1	7	6
2	11	4	12	3	0	2	3	7	2	9	3
3	7	2	13	2	0	3	2	8	3	5	1
4	6	4	14	1	0	4	4	7	4	4	0
5	7	3	15	4	1	5	6	7	5	2	2
6	6	2	16	2	....	6	2	6	6	......	1
7	8	0	17	0	....	7	6	2	7	......	1
8	2	2	18	1	....	8	9	11	8	......	....
9	7	2	19	1	....	9	5	3	9	......	....
150	4	0	Total	116	96	130	8	5	Total	117	97
1	2	1				1	7	3			
2	3	1				2	8	2			
3	2	0				3	6	1			
4	1	1				4	6	1			
5	1	....				5	6	1			
6	0	....				6	2	0			
7	1	....				7	2	1			
8	1	....				8	1	0			
9	2	....				9	1	1			
Total	116	97				140	2	1			
						1	0	....			
						2	1	....			
						3	1	....			
						4	0	....			
						5	1	....			
						6	0	....			
						7	1	....			
						8	......	....			
						9	......	....			
						Total	116	97			

Sullivan—Tongan Somatology

9. NOSE WIDTH

Millimeters	Male	Female
30	......	....
1	......	....
2	......	....
3	......	....
4	......	....
5	......	....
6	......	1
7	......	4
8	1	10
9	7	6
40	3	10
1	9	11
2	12	15
3	10	13
4	22	10
5	15	5
6	9	6
7	10	3
8	8	2
9	6	0
50	3	1
1	1	....
2	0	....
3	0	....
4	0	....
5	1	....
6	......	....
7	......	....
8	......	....
9	......	....
Total	117	97

10. EAR HEIGHT

Millimeters	Male	Female
50	......	....
1	......	....
2	......	....
3	......	....
4	......	....
5	......	....
6	2	1
7	2	1
8	2	2
9	2	3
60	3	9
1	2	8
2	14	6
3	8	13
4	13	9
5	9	12
6	9	5
7	12	6
8	11	6
9	4	3
70	7	5
1	4	2
2	5	2
3	0	2
4	1	1
5	4	1
6	0	....
7	1	....
8	0	....
9	1	....
80	1	....
1	......	....
2	......	....
3	......	....
4	......	....
5	......	....
Total	117	97

11. EAR WIDTH

Millimeters	Male	Female
20	......	....
1	......	....
2	......	....
3	......	....
4	......	....
5	1	....
6	0	....
7	0	....
8	1	....
9	1	3
30	5	9
1	4	7
2	7	19
3	18	12
4	25	18
5	13	11
6	16	11
7	10	2
8	9	2
9	3	2
40	2	0
1	0	1
2	1	....
3	......	....
4	......	....
5	......	....
6	......	....
7	......	....
8	......	....
9	......	....
Total	116	97

12. CEPHALIC INDEX

Index	Male	Female
70	......	....
1	......	....
2	......	....
3	1	....
4	2	2
5	0	2
6	5	8
7	3	4
8	10	8
9	15	8
80	19	9
1	13	10
2	12	9
3	14	9
4	6	5
5	6	4
6	3	6
7	4	4
8	2	4
9	2	2
90	......	0
1	......	2
2	......	1
3	......	....
4	......	....
5	......	....
Total	117	97

13. FRONTO-PARIETAL

Index	Male	Female
55	......	....
6	......	....
7	......	....
8	......	....
9	2	....
60	1	....
1	2	1
2	4	1
3	3	2
4	6	6
5	11	2
6	17	15
7	9	11
8	14	10
9	12	12
70	11	8
1	10	12
2	7	5
3	4	3
4	2	6
5	0	0
6	0	2
7	0	1
8	0	....
9	0	....
80	0	....
1	0	....
2	1	....
3	......	....
4	......	....
Total	116	97

14. CEPHALO-FACIAL

Index	Male	Female
80	......	....
1	......	....
2	......	....
3	......	....
4	......	2
5	1	2
6	2	3
7	2	5
8	6	10
9	6	9
90	13	9
1	14	11
2	19	8
3	8	11
4	15	14
5	4	3
6	6	4
7	10	5
8	2	0
9	4	0
100	2	1
1	0	....
2	1	....
3	1	....
4	......	....
Total	116	97

15. ZYGOMATICO-FRONTAL

Index	Male	Female
60	......	....
1	......	....
2	......	....
3	3	....
4	0	....
5	1	....
6	4	1
7	2	0
8	6	1
9	3	1
70	14	3
1	6	3
2	15	9
3	10	11
4	11	7
5	9	15
6	8	15
7	5	10
8	5	6
9	6	3
80	5	5
1	0	3
2	1	2
3	1	1
4	1	0
5	......	0
6	......	1
7	......	....
8	......	....
9	......	....
Total	116	97

16. ZYGOMATICO-MANDIBULAR

Index	Male	Female
60	......	....
1	......	....
2	......	....
3	1	....
4	2	3
5	3	....
6	1	2
7	4	3
8	4	4
9	7	7
70	7	9
1	12	13
2	10	8
3	11	9
4	17	9
5	6	11
6	5	4
7	10	6
8	4	4
9	2	5
80	0	....
1	5	....
2	1	....
3	1	....
4	0	....
5	1	....
6	1	....
7	1	....
8	......	....
9	......	....
Total	116	97

17. ANATOMICAL FACE HEIGHT

Index	Male	Female
70	......	....
1	......	....
2	......	....
3	......	....
4	......	....
5	......	....
6	......	....
7	......	....
8	2	....
9	0	....
80	2	....
1	2	....
2	2	....
3	2	1
4	6	1
5	3	5
6	10	9
7	14	5
8	5	9
9	11	11
90	13	8
1	9	9
2	10	10
3	4	6
4	10	5
5	2	5
6	5	4
7	2	2
8	......	1
9	......	0
100	......	0
1	......	2
2	2	2
3	......	0
4	......	....
5	......	....
6	......	0
7	......	1
8	......	....
9	......	....
Total	116	97

18. NASAL INDEX

Index	Male	Female
60	......	....
1	1	....
2	0	....
3	1	....
4	1	2
5	2	1
6	5	7
7	0	4
8	5	7
9	2	1
70	4	8
1	6	11
2	2	5
3	6	6
4	3	3
5	6	5
6	6	5
7	7	4
8	5	3
9	8	3
80	10	5
1	7	3
2	7	4
3	2	1
4	4	3
5	2	1
6	1	0
7	4	3
8	1	1
9	3	1
90	0	....
1	2	....
2	1	....
3	0	....
4	0	....
5	0	....
6	1	....
7	0	....
8	1	....
9	......	....
100	......	....
106	1	....
Total	117	97

19. EAR INDEX

Index	Male	Female
40	1	....
1	0	....
2	1	....
3	0	1
4	1	0
5	1	2
6	2	6
7	5	4
8	5	9
9	9	9
50	11	7
1	10	4
2	16	16
3	11	10
4	9	8
5	6	5
6	13	5
7	4	3
8	3	3
9	1	3
60	5	2
1	2	1
2	......	0
3	......	1
Total	116	97

244 Memoirs Bernice P. Bishop Museum

TABLE II.—SUMMARY OF ANTHROPOMETRIC CHARACTERS OF TONGANS

CHARACTER	MALE 92 to 117 persons				FEMALE 88 to 97 persons			
	Average	E[a]	S. D.	V	Average	E[a]	S. D.	V
1 Stature	173.0	.54	5.21	3.01	162.5	.62	5.83	3.58
2 Head length	191.0	.63	6.89	3.60	184.1	.65	6.47	3.51
3 Head width	154.8	.39	4.26	2.75	150.0	.51	5.06	3.37
4 Min. frontal	104.8	.45	4.87	4.64	103.0	.47	4.65	4.51
5 Face width	143.5	.55	5.94	4.13	136.1	.61	6.03	4.43
6 Bigonial	104.8	.54	5.81	5.54	99.2	.49	4.80	4.83
7 Face height	128.2	.63	6.81	5.31	124.1	.58	5.79	4.66
8 Nose height	57.5	.36	3.91	6.80	56.7	.38	3.75	6.61
9 Nose width	44.4	.27	3.02	6.80	41.9	.29	2.86	6.82
10 Ear height	66.0	.42	4.57	6.92	64.5	.40	3.97	6.15
11 Ear width	34.5	.24	2.62	7.59	33.4	.23	2.35	7.03
12 Cephalic index	81.1	.29	3.14	3.87	81.6	.41	4.09	5.01
13 Fronto-parietal index	67.6	.32	3.51	5.19	68.7	.32	3.22	4.68
14 Cephalo-facial index	92.8	.43	4.68	5.04	91.2	.32	3.23	3.54
15 Zygomatico-frontal index	73.1	.39	4.23	5.78	75.4	.33	3.33	4.41
16 Zygomatico mandibular index	73.2	.42	4.56	6.22	72.5	.36	3.57	4.92
17 Facial index	89.2	.41	4.43	4.96	90.8	.43	4.32	4.75
18 Nasal index	77.6	.70	7.58	9.76	74.2	.62	6.15	8.28
19 Ear index	52.4	.36	3.93	7.50	51.8	.39	3.93	7.58

[a] In this table E = propable error of the average, S. D. = standard deviation, and V = coefficient of variation in percentage.

TABLE III.—SUMMARY OF ATTRIBUTE CHARACTERS OF TONGANS

CHARACTER	MALE		FEMALE	
Skin Color:		Von Luschan's scale		
Unexposed	Nos. 14, 15, 16		Nos. 13, 14, 15, 16	
Exposed	Nos. 15, 16, 17, 18, 22, 23		Nos. 15, 16, 17, 18, 22	

Hair form:	Number	Per cent	Number	Per cent
Straight	49	41.5	33	34.4
Low waves	49	41.5	45	46.9
Deep waves	17	14.4	12	12.5
Curly	3	2.5	5	5.2
Frizzly	0	0	1	1.0
Woolly	0	0	0	0
Totals	118		96	

Hair color:	Number	Per cent	Number	Per cent
Black	111	94.1	85	87.6
Dark brown	5	4.2	4	4.1
Reddish brown	1[a]	.8	7[a]	7.2
Light brown	0	0	0	0
Blond	0	0	0	0
Golden	0	0	0	0
Red	1[a]	.8	0	0
Gray	0	0	1	1.0
Totals	118		97	

[a] Bleached with lime.

[14]

Sullivan—Tongan Somatology

CHARACTER	MALES ONLY		
Amount of Beard:	Upper cheek	Lower cheek	Chin
None	2.1	4.2	0
Scant	15.8	37.2	19.4
Medium	33.7	18.1	30.6
Heavy	48.4	40.4	50.0

	On chest	On forearm	On legs
Amount of body hair:			
None	23.4	0	0
Scant	28.7	10.5	7.3
Medium	25.5	43.2	66.7
Heavy	22.3	46.3	26.0

	MALE		FEMALE	
Eye color:	Number	Per cent	Number	Per cent
Black	4	3.4	15	15.5
Dark brown	111	94.1	79	81.4
Light brown	3	2.5	2	2.1
Blue	0	0	1	1.0
Gray	0	0	0	0
Blue-brown	0	0	0	0
Gray-brown	0	0	0	0
Total	118		97	
Conjunctiva	Number	Per cent	Number	Per cent
Clear	22	18.8	41	42.7
Not clear	95	81.2	55	57.3
Total	117		96	
Epicanthic eye fold	Number	Per cent	Number	Per cent
Absent	63	56.8	52	53.6
Trace	33	29.7	26	26.8
Medium	9	8.1	14	14.4
Marked	6	5.4	5	5.2
Total	111		97	
Nasal bridge	Number	Per cent	Number	Per cent
Low	21	21.7	29	30.5
Medium	81	70.4	64	67.4
High	9	7.8	2	2.1
Total	111		95	
Axes of nostrils a	Number	Per cent	Number	Per cent
Anterior-posterior	2	1.7	5	5.3
Oblique	90	78.3	66	69.5
Transverse	23	20.0	24	25.3
Total	115		95	
Slope of forehead	Number	Per cent	Number	Per cent
Vertical	70	60.3	81	84.4
Moderate	45	38.8	15	15.6
Low	1	.9	0	0
Total	116		96	

a See figs. 1 and 2.

Memoirs Bernice P. Bishop Museum

CHARACTER	MALE		FEMALE	
Glabella	Number	Per cent	Number	Per cent
Smooth	55	49.1	81	83.5
Medium	48	42.8	15	15.5
Prominent	9	8.0	1	1.0
Total	112		97	
Lips	Number	Per cent	Number	Per cent
Thin	12	10.3	10	10.3
Medium	97	83.6	85	87.6
Thick	7	6.0	2	2.1
Total	116		97	
Prognathism	Number	Per cent	Number	Per cent
None	63	53.3	45	46.4
Slight	26	22.0	36	37.1
Medium	29	24.6	15	15.5
Marked	0	0	1	1.0
Total	118		97	
Ear lobe	Number	Per cent	Number	Per cent
None	5	4.3	2	2.1
Small separate	48	41.7	37	38.5
Small attached	48	41.7	44	45.8
Large separate	9	7.8	8	8.3
Large attached	5	4.3	5	5.2
Total	115		96	
Helix roll	Number	Per cent	Number	Per cent
Flat	0	0	2	2.1
Rolled first ⅓	20	16.1	34	35.4
Rolled first ⅔	67	56.8	48	50.0
Rolled throughout	31	26.3	12	12.5
Total	118		96	
Darwin's tubercle	Number	Per cent	Number	Per cent
Present	25	21.4	5	5.2
Keilodonty	Number	Per cent	Number	Per cent
Lateral incisor teeth				
No rim	48	42.1	33	36.3
Trace of rim	49	42.9	37	40.6
Medium rim / Marked rim \	17	14.9	21	23.1
Mesial incisor teeth				
No rim	66	57.9	57	62.6
Trace of rim	34	29.8	24	26.4
Medium rim / Marked rim \	14	12.3	10	10.9
Total	114		91	

[16]

The results summarized in Tables II and III show that the Tongans are among the tallest groups of mankind. The men average 173 centimeters or about 5 feet 8 inches in height. On the average the women are 10 centimeters, or 4 inches, shorter. The head is both long and broad yielding an average index of 81.1 for the men and 81.6 for the women. There is no assurance, however, that these are the natural diameters of the Tongan head. In the skeletal material brought back by Gifford and McKern, seven crania were in a fair state of preservation. With the single exception of one cranium of a young child all of these crania showed a moderate to a pronounced degree of occipital flattening accompanied by marked asymmetry, pointing clearly to the fact that they had been artificially deformed. The cranial length-breadth indices were 82.7, 84.5, 86.0, 86.0, 88.2, and 93.7. These average 86.8.

At my request inquiries were made by Gifford and McKern as to the prevalence and methods of head deformation. The information shows that the Tongans in the past and to some extent at the present time shape the heads of children, but the description of the methods employed throws no light on the deformation seen in the crania. According to several informants the child was laid on a piece of tapa with the top of its head placed against a heavy block of squared wood, the pressure tending to flatten the top of the cranium. The deformation described above is decidedly not of this type. Since this procedure is said to have been continued for one month only, its effect may be considered as negligible. It is difficult to understand how it would have any appreciable effect even if continued indefinitely, since the amount of pressure involved must have been very slight.

In the Tongan skeletal material that I examined, the tops of the crania show no evidences of flattening. The deformation on these Tongan crania is very similar to that observed in the crania of many groups of Indians in the southwestern United States. Occipital flattening is usually thought to be accidental—at least in origin. When the effect of it was once recognized, conscious effort may have been made in certain groups to duplicate by artificial means the results obtained by accident. The hard beds and wooden pillows that are still in use among the Tongans suggest a possible explanation of the occipital flattening, as it is known that a certain amount of deformation or flattening is easily brought about by hard pillows, particularly in persons who are naturally short headed. Examples of such accidental flattening of the occiput are numerous among the Chinese, Japanese, and Koreans. The only difficulty involved in this explanation is to account for the difference between the degree of deformation found in the living series and that in the cranial series. It is known that the crania are not modern. The average length-breadth index of these crania is nearly 6 points higher than the same index in the living. On the whole, while the implication is that deformation is not so prevalent at present as in the past, it seems better to base no generalization on the form of the head. Directly or indirectly, minimum frontal diameter, transverse fronto-parietal index and cephalo-facial index would also be somewhat altered in persons with deformed occiputs. On account of the very close correspondence of Tongans and Samoans in cephalic index it is obvious that this caution should be extended to the Samoan data[5] as well.

The transverse and vertical diameters of the Tongan face and its component parts are so large that the face and nose may both well be described as massive. The skin is a medium yellowish-brown where it is unexposed to wind and sun.

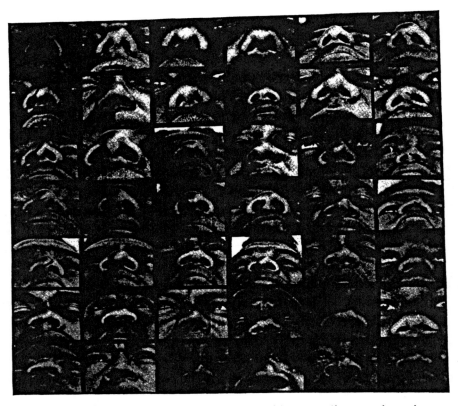

FIGURE 2. Tongan nostrils arranged roughly according to the orientation of the axes. Photographs by Gifford and McKern.

Exposed parts of the skin of a few of the persons were a very dark chocolate-brown. The hair may be described as black, of medium coarseness, and either straight or slightly waved. The beard is moderately developed and the amount of body-hair on the chest, arms, and legs may also be described as somewhat below the average. The eyes are dark brown in color and a considerable amount of conjunctival pigment is normal. The epicanthic eye fold is typically absent, but nearly 30 per cent showed what is termed a "trace" of this fold, and a few marked examples of it were noted.

---
[5] B. P. Bishop Mus. Mem. vol. VIII, No. 2, 1921.

The eyes of Tongans as a group are less wide open than are the eyes of Caucasian peoples. The types illustrated in Nos. 3, 4, 5, and 6 in Plate xxxvi, *A*, are most common. They are characterized by being placed somewhat obliquely with just a suggestion of an epicanthic fold, and by a slightly thickened and bevelled lower lid. No. 8 has a well-marked epicanthic fold and No. 7 a definite trace of it.

The nose of the Tongan is worthy of some detailed description and comparison. As judged by the standard of the European nose the nasal bridge of Tongans cannot be said to be highly arched. (See Pl. xxxviii, *A* and *B*.) It is prevailingly of medium or low elevation from the face. The nostrils are somewhat oval in shape with the long axis tending to run in an oblique or transverse direction.

Although, as expressed by the nasal index, the Tongan has what is usually termed a moderately broad or mesorrhine nose, yet by absolute measurement the nasal width is exceeded only by that of a few Negroid groups. (See Pls. xxxvi and xxxix.) In Table IV I have given some comparative data on the range of the nasal index for given widths of nose. It is not at all unusual to find groups with identical nasal widths varying by 20 points in nasal index. This leads me to believe that unless the absolute diameters are somewhat nearly alike in two groups a correspondence in nasal index should not be taken too seriously. The enormous proportions of the Tongan (and also of the Samoan) nose are approached only by certain American Indian groups. The Tongans, the Samoans, the Chippewa Indians, the Egyptians, the Ilokos, the Kirghez, the Khotan, and the Polish Jews have nasal indices averaging from 72.6 to 78.0. Does it follow that their noses are very similar? Not at all. In some cases the low nasal index is the result of the great height of the nose and in spite of the great width. This is true of the Tongans, Samoans, and Chippewa Indians. In the others it is due to the fact that the noses are of moderate width and height. So it seems that the use of the nasal index should at least be supplemented by absolute measurements.

250   *Memoirs Bernice P. Bishop Museum*

TABLE IV. COMPARISON OF NASAL WIDTH, NASAL HEIGHT, AND NASAL INDICES ARRANGED IN ORDER OF MAGNITUDE OF NASAL WIDTH.

GROUP	NASAL WIDTH	NASAL HEIGHT	NASAL INDEX	AUTHOR
Kajji, Nigeria	45.0	49.0	91.0	Tremearne
Mawambi pygmy	45.0	......	......	Martin
Tonga	44.4	57.5	77.6	Sullivan
Toricelli, New Guinea	44.3	......	......	Martin
Fan	44.0	48.0	91.1	Martin
Kagoro, Nigeria	44.0	47.0	92.9	Tremearne
Sentani, New Guinea	44.0	49.0	87.9	Van der Sande
Humboldt Bay, New Guinea	44.0	53.0	83.7	Van der Sande
Samoa	43.8	59.8	73.6	Sullivan
Shoshoni Amerindian	43.4	52.2	83.1	Boas
Chippewa Amerindian	42.8	56.5	75.5	Hrdlicka
Negrito, Zambales	42.8	40.5	106.0	Reed
Maricopa Amerindian	41.4	49.0	85.2	Ten Kate
Tagalog Bulakan	41.0	50.0	82.0	Folkmar
Tagalog, Rizal	41.0	51.0	80.5	Folkmar
Bisaya Iloilo	41.0	49.0	84.1	Folkmar
Nahuqua Amerindian	40.5	......	......	Martin
Iloko, Ilokos Norte	40.0	55.0	73.1	Folkmar
Senoi	40.0	47.0	85.0	Martin
Dolan, Turkestan	39.9	51.2	78.9	Joyce
Subanun	39.9	52.6	74.8	Christie
Sioux Amerindian	39.9	58.3	68.8	Sullivan
Sundanese	39.0	45.1	86.9	Garrett
Banjerese	38.8	44.3	88.0	Garrett
Kirghiz	38.2	49.3	78.1	Joyce
Dombs, India	38.0	44.0	86.5	Fawcett
Aino	38.0	55.9	68.0	Koganei
Nabaloi, Benguet	38.0	40.0	95.0	Bean
South Andamanese	37.7	42.7	88.2	Martin
Egyptian	37.3	48.7	76.6	Martin
Polish Jew	37.0	51.0	72.6	Fishberg
Little Russian Jew	37.0	53.0	69.8	Fishberg
Khotan, Turkestan	36.9	49.9	74.7	Joyce

The forehead of the Tongan is well developed and presents a rather gradual slope. The glabella is developed only to a moderate degree. Though the lips are designated as of medium thickness (Pl. xxxvi, *B*), it is obvious that if our standards were more sensitive we should find that they were somewhat above the average in thickness. As a group the Tongans are not prognathous. However it is safe to say that the face is more projecting than that of the European. The chin is positive but not so prominent a feature as that of Europeans. (See Pl. xxxvii, *A* and xxxvii, *B*.) The ears are large but offer no points of special interest. The rim on the lingual surface of the upper incisor teeth is typically not well developed. It was noticed, however, in what may be termed a moderate degree of frequency.

[20]

COMPARISON OF THE TONGANS WITH THE SAMOANS

Researches during the past year provide the necessary data for a comparison of the Tongans and the Samoans, and it is practicable to make the comparison somewhat more detailed than is usual, because both groups were studied by the same men, and differences in method and technique can therefore be largely ignored.

In Table V the standard deviations and coefficients of variation are compared. The Samoan series is somewhat noteworthy for its relative homogeneity when compared with existing groups of man. As a group the Tongans show noticeably more variation than the Samoans. In thirteen of the nineteen characters under discussion the Tongans are more variable than the Samoans—a statement which applies to both sexes. In the six characters in which the Samoans exceed the Tongans in range, the excess is very slight. In most of the characters in which the Tongans are the more variable the excess is appreciably larger. In both groups the variability as expressed by the coefficient of variation is considerably greater in the males than in the females.

In comparing the averages of the two groups for each anthropometric character shown in Table VI and the frequencies of the attribute characters shown in Table VII, the very close correspondence of the Tongans to the Samoans is striking in every character that lends itself to accurate measurement. Most of the differences occurring might well be regarded as chance differences. It must be remembered again that small differences in distribution in the attribute or descriptive characters are not to be taken too seriously.

TABLE V. COMPARISON OF STANDARD DEVIATIONS AND COEFFICIENTS OF VARIATION IN SAMOAN AND TONGAN SERIES

CHARACTER	MALE				FEMALE			
	S. D. ±		V. in per cent		S. D. ±		V. in per cent	
	Samoan	Tongan	Samoan	Tongan	Samoan	Tongan	Samoan	Tongan
1. Stature	5.25	5.21	3.05	3.01	4.92	5.83	3.05	3.58
2. Head length	5.69	6.89	2.98	3.60	5.22	6.47	2.85	3.51
3. Head width	4.46	4.26	2.88	2.75	3.87	5.06	2.61	3.37
4. Minimum frontal	5.98	4.87	5.78	4.64	3.96	4.65	3.90	4.51
5. Face width	5.23	5.94	3.59	4.13	3.79	6.03	2.77	4.43
6. Bigonial	5.13	5.81	4.90	5.54	3.93	4.80	3.96	4.83
7. Face height	6.56	6.81	5.00	5.31	6.41	5.79	5.30	4.66
8. Nose height	3.64	3.91	6.09	6.80	4.53	3.75	8.34	6.61
9. Nose width	2.59	3.02	5.91	6.80	2.56	2.86	6.21	6.82
10. Ear height	4.23	4.57	6.39	6.92	3.33	3.97	5.44	6.15
11. Ear width	2.76	2.62	7.84	7.59	2.30	2.35	6.84	7.03
12. Cephalic index	3.53	3.14	4.34	3.87	2.98	4.09	3.68	5.01
13. Fronto-parietal index	3.30	3.51	4.94	5.19	3.12	3.22	4.54	4.68
14. Cephalo-facial index	2.84	4.68	3.01	5.04	2.63	3.23	2.84	3.54
15. Zygomatico-frontal index	3.55	4.23	5.01	5.78	3.34	3.33	4.49	4.41
16. Zygomatico-mandibular index	3.84	4.56	5.42	6.22	3.50	3.57	4.83	4.92
17. Facial index	4.87	4.43	5.42	4.96	5.03	4.32	5.60	4.75
18. Nasal index	5.86	7.58	7.96	9.76	7.99	6.15	10.47	8.28
19. Ear index	3.79	3.93	7.11	7.50	4.53	3.93	8.25	7.58

[21]

Memoirs Bernice P. Bishop Museum

TABLE VI. COMPARISON OF AVERAGES OF ANTHROPOMETRIC CHARACTERS OF TONGANS AND SAMOANS

CHARACTER	MALE				FEMALE		
	1	2	3	4	5	6	7
	A_1	A_2	A_1-A_2	$\sqrt{e_1^2 + e_2^2}$	A_1	A_2	A_1-A_2
	Samoan 67–70 Persons	Tongan 92–117 Persons			Samoan 20–23 Persons	Tongan 88–97 Persons	
1. Stature	171.7	173.0	+ 1.3	.83	161.2	162.5	+ 1.3
2. Head length	190.6	191.0	+ 0.4	.93	183.0	184.1	+ 1.1
3. Head width	154.8	154.8	0.0	.67	148.1	150.0	+ 1.9
4. Minimum frontal	103.4	104.8	+ 1.4	.85	101.5	103.0	+ 1.5
5. Face width	145.9	143.5	— 2.4[2]	.84	136.5	136.1	— 0.4
6. Bigonial	104.6	104.8	+ 0.2	.82	99.0	99.2	+ 0.2
7. Face height	131.1	128.2	— 2.9[2]	1.01	121.1	124.1	+ 3.0
8. Nose height	59.8	57.5	— 2.3[1]	.56	54.3	56.7	+ 2.4
9. Nose width	43.8	44.4	+ 0.6	.41	41.2	41.9	+ 0.7
10. Ear height	66.1	66.0	— 0.1	.65	61.2	64.5	+ 3.3
11. Ear width	35.2	34.5	— 0.7	.41	33.6	33.4	— 0.2
12. Cephalic index	81.3	81.1	— 0.2	.51	80.8	81.6	+ 0.8
13. Fronto-parietal index	66.8	67.6	+ 0.8	.51	68.8	68.7	— 0.1
14. Cephalo-facial index	94.2	92.8	— 1.4[2]	.55	92.4	91.2	— 1.2
15. Zygomatico-frontal index	70.9	73.1	+ 2.2[1]	.58	74.5	75.4	+ 0.9
16. Zygomatico-mandibular index	71.7	73.2	+ 1.5	.62	72.5	72.5	0.0
17. Facial index	89.9	89.2	— 0.7	.72	89.8	90.8	+ 1.0
18. Nasal index	73.6	77.6	+ 4.0[1]	.99	76.3	74.2	— 2.1
19. Ear index	53.3	52.4	— 0.9	.58	54.9	51.8	— 3.1

In Table VI the Samoan male averages are given in column 1 and the Tongan male averages in column 2. The differences of the two averages with the Samoans as a standard are given in column 3, superior figure 1 indicating possible significant difference and superior figure 2 an approach to significant difference. These differences are compared with the magnitude of the errors of the averages in column 4. Unless a difference in column 3 is three times as great as the magnitude of the errors in column 4, it is not regarded as significant. Columns 5, 6, and 7 give the same data for the females as are given in columns 1, 2, and 3 for males The differences in the females are less significant on account of the size of the Samoan sample.

TABLE VII. COMPARISON OF ATTRIBUTE CHARACTERS IN TONGANS AND SAMOANS ON A PERCENTAGE BASIS

CHARACTER	MALE		FEMALE	
	Samoan 67–70 Persons	Tongan 92–118 Persons	Samoan 20–23 Persons	Tongan 88–97 Persons
Skin color (unexposed part)	Medium brown	Medium brown	Medium brown	Medium brown
Von Luschan's numbers	14, 15, 16	14, 15, 16, 17	13, 14, 15	13, 14, 15, 16

[22]

Sullivan—Tongan Somatology

CHARACTER	MALE		FEMALE	
	Samoan	Tongan	Samoan	Tongan
Hair form				
Straight	55.1	41.5	47.8	34.4
Low waves	27.5	41.5	39.1	46.9
Deep waves	10.1	14.4	8.8	12.5
Curly	5.8	2.5	0	5.2
Frizzly	1.4	0	4.3	1.0
Woolly	0	0	0	0

Hair color				
Black	91.4	94.1	56.9	87.6
Dark brown	4.3	4.2	8.8	4.1

Amount of hair—males only	UPPER CHEEK		CHIN	
None	10.1	2.1	0	0
Scant	46.3	15.8	23.2	19.4
Medium	31.9	33.7	27.5	30.6
Heavy	11.5	48.4	49.2	50.0

	LOWER CHEEK		CHEST	
None	14.5	4.2	59.7	23.4
Scant	43.3	37.2	22.3	28.7
Medium	23.2	18.1	14.9	25.5
Heavy	18.8	40.4	3.0	22.3

	FOREARM		LEG	
None	3.0	0	0	0
Scant	19.1	10.5	7.2	7.3
Medium	35.3	43.2	42.0	66.7
Heavy	42.6	46.3	50.7	26.0

	MALE		FEMALE	
Eye color				
Black	2.9	3.4	13.0	15.5
Dark brown	97.1	94.1	82.6	81.4
Light brown	0	2.5	4.3	2.1
Blue	0	0	0	1.0

Conjunctiva				
Clear	23.5	18.8	45.4	42.7
Not clear	76.5	81.2	54.6	57.3

Epicanthic eye fold				
Absent	68.1	56.8	47.8	53.6
Trace	27.5	29.7	43.4	26.8
Medium	2.8	8.1	8.8	14.4
Marked	1.4	5.4	0	5.2

Nasal bridge				
Low	21.4	21.7	56.9	30.5
Medium	64.3	70.4	39.1	67.4
High	14.3	7.8	4.3	2.1

CHARACTER	MALE		FEMALE	
	Samoan	Tongan	Samoan	Tongan
Axes of nostrils				
Anterior posterior	2.9	1.7	0	5.3
Oblique	57.3	78.3	39.1	69.5
Transverse	39.7	20.0	60.9	25.3
Slope of forehead				
Vertical	40.0	60.3	85.7	84.4
Moderate	58.5	38.8	14.3	15.6
Low	1.5	.9	0	0
Glabella				
Smooth	29.4	49.1	100.0	83.5
Medium	55.8	42.8	0	15.5
Prominent	14.7	8.0	0	1.0
Lips				
Thin	0	10.3	4.3	10.3
Medium	92.8	83.6	91.4	87.6
Thick	7.1	6.0	4.3	2.1
Prognathism				
None	56.7	53.3	69.6	46.4
Slight	23.8	22.0	13.0	37.1
Medium	17.8	24.6	17.4	15.5
Marked	1.4	0	0	1.0
Keilodonty				
Lateral incisor teeth:				
No rim	51.5	42.1	57.1	36.3
Trace of rim	34.3	42.9	23.8	40.6
Medium rim} Marked rim}	14.1	14.9	19.0	23.1
Mesial incisor teeth:				
No rim	68.2	57.9	76.0	62.6
Trace of rim	25.7	29.8	14.3	26.4
Medium rim} Marked rim}	6.0	12.3	9.5	10.9

Although the differences are small it may be profitable to further analyze those that do occur. Head length and breadth and, consequently, the cephalic index are almost identical in the two groups, but the Tongans have slightly lower, narrower faces, lower noses, a higher average nasal index and lower average cephalofacial indices. There is also noticeable a slightly greater tendency to have wavy or curly hair. Beards are slightly heavier and body hair more plentiful. There is more conjunctival pigment in the Tongans and a higher frequency of the epicanthic eye fold. There are fewer highly arched nasal bridges.

EVIDENCES OF MELANESIAN INTERMIXTURE

Although the differences between Tongans and Samoans are very slight, yet almost without exception they point in the direction of Melanesia. Of the Samoans[6] I said that considering the group as a unit there seems to be very little Melanesian blood in evidence. On the basis of cultural or linguistic affinities it is common to assume a large amount of Melanesian blood in all Polynesian groups. If such blood exists it should be easily demonstrable. Melanesian intermixture should result in a lower stature, longer heads, broader, shorter noses, shorter ears, more curly, frizzly, or woolly hair, more beard and body hair, a smaller transverse fronto-parietal index, a lower, narrower face, greater prognathism, and a heavier development of the glabella and supra-orbital region. A large percentage of the difference between Tongans and Samoans is of a nature that from purely theoretical reasons I suggested might be expected to result from Melanesian mixture. As a matter of fact there are few or no careful and detailed descriptions of those Melanesian groups that are geographically nearest to the Tongans and very meager data from the area as a whole. In order to state with any finality what might be expected from the mixture of Polynesians and Melanesians, in lieu of any absolute data on the question, detailed and accurate descriptions of several living Melanesian groups would at least be necessary.

Assuming, however, that I have stated with approximate accuracy what might be expected in such a mixture, the analysis can be carried a step further. As a test woolly, frizzly, curly, deeply waved, and, to a less extent, low-waved hair, may be taken to indicate Melanesian physical mixture. If it does indicate Melanesian mixture and this mixture has taken place on a large scale within fairly recent times, it is to be expected that persons with wavy and curly hair will show other Melanesian characteristics. By this I do not mean that there is necessarily any high correlation between the combinations in which physical characters are inherited when two races mix but that, purely on the basis of chance, if curly, wavy hair indicates the presence of Melanesian blood, it is reasonable to expect that the curly, wavy-haired group, as a unit, will show a closer approach to the Melanesian average than will the straight-haired group.

Accordingly I have divided my material on the basis of hair form into three groups. The first group includes the straight-haired persons, the second group those with low waved hair, and the third group includes all with deeply-waved, curly, or frizzly hair. I have compared these three groups with the total series. The averages of the three groups do not necessarily equal the averages of the total series since the data for a number of persons who were doubtfully marked "straight to low waves" or "low waves to deep waves" were excluded in making up the

---

[6] Op. cit., p. 96.

256 — Memoirs Bernice P. Bishop Museum

smaller groups. In seriating these doubtful types of hair form in the summary, I alternately placed one of these in the lower class and one in the upper class. In obtaining averages of groups based on hair form, it seemed best to exclude the data marked "doubtful." The averages for the anthropometric characters in these four groups will be found in Table VIII.

TABLE VIII.—AVERAGES OF ANTHROPOMETRIC CHARACTERS FOR TONGANS WITH DIFFERENT TYPES OF HAIR FORM

MEN

Character	Total group	Straight hair	Low-waved hair	Deep-waved to woolly hair
1. Stature	173.0	171.0	173.9	173.2
2. Head length	191.0	189.3	193.2	192.2
3. Head width	154.8	154.3	155.2	156.9
4. Minimum frontal	104.8	102.4	106.1	103.3
5. Face width	143.5	144.7	145.2	143.9
7. Face height	128.2	129.7	129.0	128.3
8. Nose height	57.5	58.9	57.8	57.0
9. Nose width	44.4	44.3	44.8	45.6
12. Cephalic index	81.1	81.3	80.3	81.8
13. Fronto-parietal index	67.6	66.3	68.3	66.0
14. Cephalo-facial index	92.8	93.7	93.7	91.9
17. Facial index	89.2	89.8	88.9	89.3
18. Nasal index	77.6	75.5	77.7	80.4

WOMEN

Character	Total group	Straight hair	Low-waved hair	Deep-waved to woolly hair
1. Stature	162.5	161.3	163.1	162.3
5. Face width	136.1	137.0	137.2	136.4
7. Face height	124.1	124.0	124.5	123.3
8. Nose height	56.7	57.3	56.8	56.1
9. Nose width	41.9	42.1	41.9	41.8
12. Cephalic index	81.6	81.0	82.2	81.2
13. Fronto-parietal index	68.7	69.1	67.9	69.3
14. Cephalo-facial index	91.2	91.5	91.0	90.9
18. Nasal index	74.2	73.6	74.2	74.7

There are no consistent differences between the straight-haired and the low-waved groups. But in the groups containing the persons with deeply waved, curly, frizzly, and woolly hair we notice that the averages again point in the direction of Melanesia. The faces are lower and narrower, the noses are lower and wider, the average cephalo-facial index is lower and the nasal index is higher.

Emphasizing, then, more the nature than the magnitude of the difference, I am inclined to believe that in those traits in which the Tongans differ from the Samoans the differences may probably be attributed to Melanesian intermixture.

DISCUSSION AND CONCLUSIONS

Comparison of the Tongans with the Samoans has thus shown remarkably close resemblance between these two groups in almost every detail. The few small differences might well be considered as accidental or as reflecting slight local differences, were it not for the fact that they point in the main in one direction. From the general direction of these differences it seems most reasonable to assume that they are the result of Melanesian intermixture.

In another publication[7] I stated that I saw no reason for assuming any appreciable amount of Melanesian blood in Samoa. Perhaps this statement should be qualified to make its meaning clearer. The census returns show that there are in Samoa and Tonga a considerable number of natives of Fiji and other Melanesian islands. In both of these island groups there are persons of known and admittedly mixed Melanesian-Polynesian parentage. These facts are known and require no anthropological research to establish them. In view of these facts it is desirable to determine to what extent the population styling itself as of pure Samoan or of pure Tongan origin has been in the past affected by Melanesian intermixture.

This problem can be solved only by determining the degrees of differences and likenesses in the groups concerned. The results, however, can be expressed only in general terms, for there are no known factors in the equation. From the marked general differences in physical type between Samoans and Melanesians I conclude that the amount of Melanesian blood in Samoa is very small. This may be due to the fact that intermixture never took place on a very large scale in Samoa, or that if it did take place on a large scale it was so long ago that the Melanesian element is almost completely absorbed by the general Samoan population.

In Tonga conditions are somewhat different. Enough Melanesian blood is in evidence to alter noticeably the average physical type. But such correlation exists between the various Melanesian traits in individuals and groups that when individuals are classed on the basis of one Melanesian trait the averages in many other traits also reflect the Melanesian intermixture more clearly than do the Tongans as a whole.

From this it may be assumed that the Melanesian element in Tonga is either comparatively recent or considerable in amount. The chances are in favor of recent rather than great intermixture, but since skeletal material of known chronological sequence is lacking, no definite conclusion is possible. It may be said, however, that without much doubt there is considerably more Melanesian blood in the general Tongan population than there is in the general Samoan population.

In their broader racial affinities the Samoans and Tongans are very similar, and therefore what I have said of the Samoans holds for the Tongans. Never-

---

[7] Op. cit.

258   *Memoirs Bernice P. Bishop Museum*

theless it seems desirable to repeat the discussion in my paper on Samoan Somatology[8] and to extend it somewhat.

I have stated my belief that there was little or no reason for assuming the Samoans to be of European or Caucasian origin. From the evidence available I have concluded that the Samoans are of Mongoloid or Yellow-Brown affinities. Scientific opinion has wavered back and forth on the question as to whether there was or was not justification for calling the yellow and the brown elements of this stock separate races. Everyone must admit that there is some justification for so doing. Superficially there are some striking differences in the two stocks. When all the groups composing this stock are considered, anthropologists have found that the two elements have a considerable number of very important characteristics in common. One group may depart radically from the other groups in one or two characters but in all other characters will approach the form prevailing in the majority of the groups. At present the line of cleavage between the yellow and brown elements of this stock seems to be rather well marked. This is probably due not to the fact that such a gap exists but that our data is lacking on many interesting and connecting types. The Chinese, the Japanese, the Koreans, the numerous Siberian peoples, and many other similar Asiatic groups constitute the yellow element of this group. The American Indians, the Malays, the Indonesians and in my opinion the Polynesians constitute the brown element of the Yellow-Brown race. Each one of these groups named represents a departure from the other groups in a greater or less number of important characteristics. Yet analysis reveals a large number of remaining characteristics pointing clearly to its major affinities.

It is for this reason that I insist that no classification based on hair form, cephalic index, or any one single character should be taken too seriously. It may very well be that the one character which was hit upon as a basis for classification may be the very one in which the group under discussion has become differentiated from its closest relatives. Relationship must be based on a totality of characters—the larger the number of physical characters used in indicating relationships the greater the probability that the relationship indicated is a real one.

The evidence for a Caucasian origin of the Samoans and Tongans is decidedly sparse and unconvincing. They do depart somewhat from the bulk of the Yellow-Brown peoples in hair form. Coarse, stiff, or lank black hair occurs only rarely in these two groups. The prevailing form is moderately coarse in texture and either straight or, quite as often, slightly wavy in form. This more than any other one thing is responsible for the theory of a European origin of these peoples. Now while the hair is not so stiff, straight, and coarse as the prevailing form of hair in the Yellow-Brown peoples, neither is it so fine as the

---

[8] Op. cit.

[28]

prevailing hair form of the Caucasians. I do not wish, however, to make too much of this point and am willing to grant that in this one character the Samoans and Tongans approach nearer to the Caucasian than to the Yellow-Brown types. The same can be said of the lack of prognathism and of the development of the chin. But it should be remembered that the Polynesians are not alone among the Yellow-Browns in thus approaching a Caucasian norm. Certain American Indians approach the Caucasian norms even more closely in the lack of prognathism, elevation of the nose, and in the development of the chin.

A few other characters upon which we have data are intermediate between the prevailing Caucasian and Yellow-Brown norms. In detail these are hair texture, amount of beard, amount of body hair, size, shape and direction of the palpebral fissure (eye opening), low frequency of the epicanthic eye fold, low frequency of the enamel rim on the upper incisor teeth, the size of the teeth, the hair color (occasionally a slight brownish tint in sunlight) and the cephalo-facial index.

But in skin color, eye color, the amount of conjunctival pigment, the elevation of the nasal bridge, the form and direction of the nostrils, nasal height, nasal breadth, nasal index, the thickness of the lips, the large massive faces reflected in the face height, face width, and bigonial width, the Samoans and the Tongans differ from the Caucasians and approach more nearly the norms of the brown division of the Yellow-Brown race. These characters may be summarized in tabular form as follows:

TABLE IX.—RACIAL AFFINITIES OF THE TONGANS AND SAMOANS

A. Approach Caucasian norms in:	B. Intermediate between Caucasian and Yellow-Brown in:	C. Approach Yellow-Brown norm in:
Hair form	Hair texture	Skin color
Lack of prognathism	Amount of beard	Eye color
Chin development	Amount of body hair	Conjunctival pigment
	Form of palpebral fissure	Nasal bridge
	Absence of eye fold	Nostrils
	Absence of incisor rim	Nasal height
	Hair color	Nasal breadth
	Cephalo-facial index	Nasal index
		Lips
		Face width
		Face height
		Bigonial diameter

It will be noted that many characters occurring in both races but distinctive of neither have been omitted. I may likewise have laid myself open to criticism by assigning any one character exclusively to one race. This has been done consciously for the sake of clearness in presentation. In saying, for example, that the Tongans and Samoans approach the norm of the Yellow-Brown race in skin color, I say it knowing that a few Caucasian groups have a skin color nearer to that of the Tongans and Samoans than to many Yellow-Brown groups. Yet on the whole brown skin is more distinctive of the Yellow-Brown peoples than it is of the Caucasians. I have also perhaps been somewhat too generous in admitting that certain characters approach the Caucasian norm when they also approach the norms of other race groups. While I have said that in the amount of beard and body hair the Samoans and Tongans approach the Caucasian norms it should be remembered that in these respects they approach just as closely the Melanesian norm.

Beyond saying that the bulk of the data at hand seems to point to the conclusion that the Polynesians under discussion belong to the brown division of the Yellow-Brown race in the same sense that it is customary to regard the American Indians as members of this race, it seems unwise to go further at this time. From this it should not be assumed that the relationship of the Polynesians and the American Indians is immediate and close. At present I would not care to do more than to express a belief that the relationship existing between the Polynesians and the American Indians is considerably closer than that existing between either the Polynesians or the American Indians and the Chinese. It is probable, however, that closer relatives to the Polynesian will be found nearer at hand.

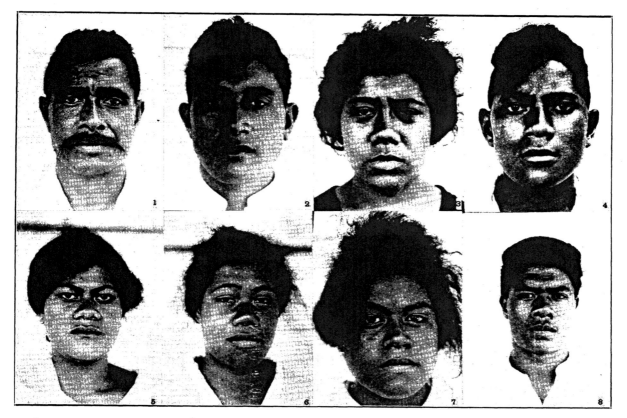

A. TONGAN TYPES SHOWING THE RANGE OF VARIATION IN EYE FORM, THE CHARACTERISTIC HALF-OPEN EYES SOMEWHAT OBLIQUELY PLACED, AND THE SLIGHTLY THICKENED AND BEVELLED LOWER LID WITH JUST A SUGGESTION OF AN EPICANTHIC FOLD.

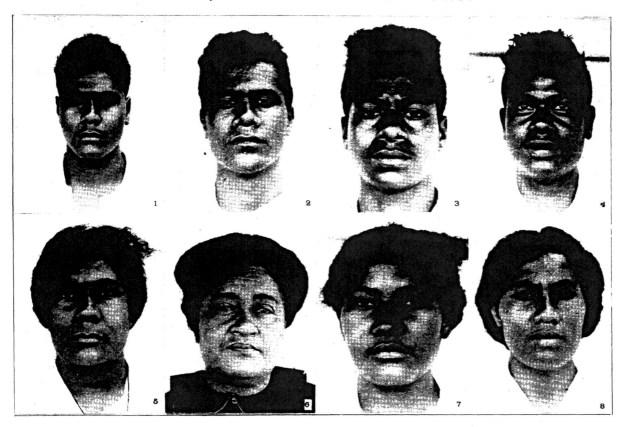

B. TONGAN TYPES SHOWING THE FORM OF THE LIPS, NOS. 1 TO 4 IN MEN AND NOS. 5 TO 8 IN WOMEN. NOS. 2, 3, 6, AND 7 ARE THE MOST COMMON TYPES. AS A GROUP THE TONGANS HAVE LIPS OF SOMEWHAT MORE THAN MEDIUM THICKNESS, DIFFERING QUITE MARKEDLY FROM THOSE OF CAUCASIAN PEOPLE.

Photographs by Gifford and McKern

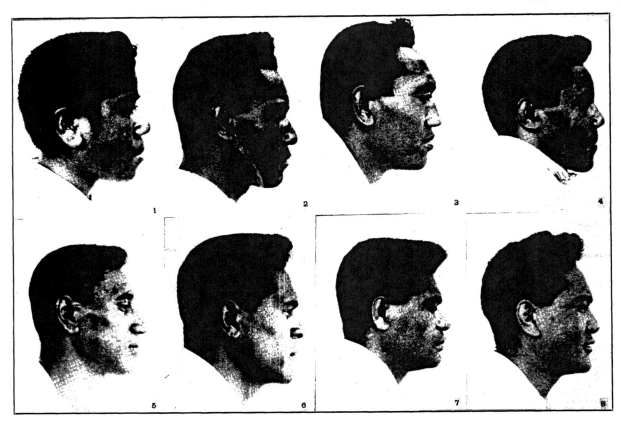

A. PROFILES OF TONGAN MEN ARRANGED IN ORDER OF CHIN DEVELOPMENT. THE TONGAN CHIN THOUGH POSITIVE IS BY NO MEANS SO PRONOUNCED AS THAT OF CAUCASIAN PEOPLES. NOS. 3, 4, 5, AND 6 PORTRAY THE MOST COMMON TYPES.

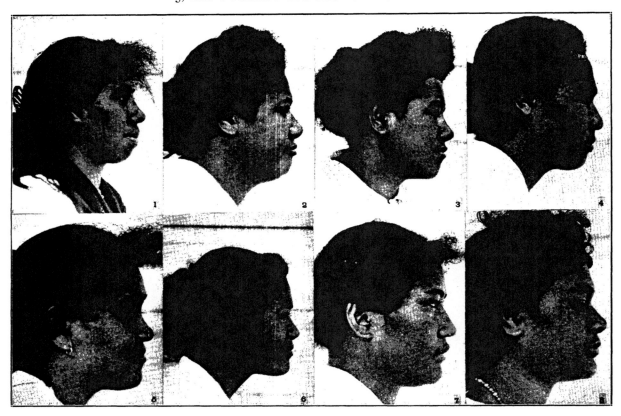

B. PROFILES OF TONGAN WOMEN ARRANGED IN ORDER OF CHIN DEVELOPMENT. THE CHIN OF TONGAN WOMEN IS NOTICEABLY LESS DEVELOPED THAN THAT OF THE MEN. NOS. 3, 4, 5, AND 6 PORTRAY THE MOST COMMON TYPES.

Photographs by Gifford and McKern

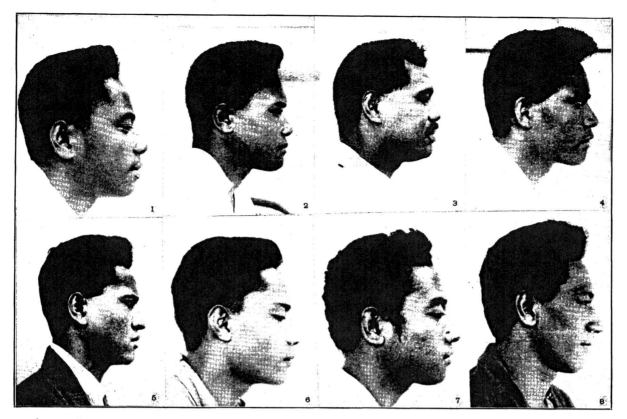

A. PROFILES OF TONGAN MEN SHOWING THE ELEVATION OF THE NASAL BRIDGE AND THE PROFILE OF THE NOSE. NOS. 7 AND 8 SHOW A HIGHLY ELEVATED NASAL BRIDGE. THE NASAL BRIDGE OF THE TONGANS AS A GROUP IS NOT ELEVATED SO MUCH AS THAT OF CAUCASIANS.

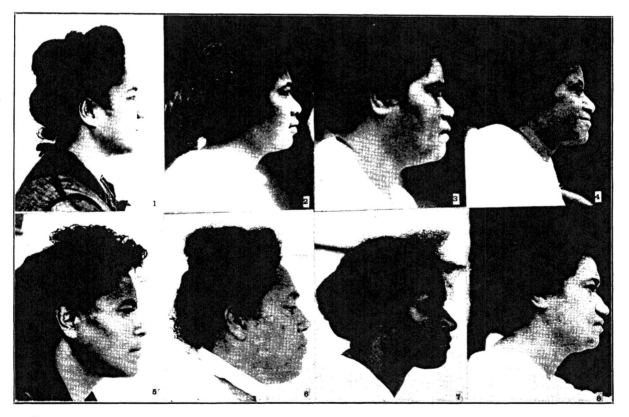

B. PROFILES OF TONGAN WOMEN SHOWING THE RANGE IN ELEVATION OF THE NASAL BRIDGE AND THE CONTOUR OF THE NASAL PROFILE. THE NASAL BRIDGE IS SEEN TO BE MODERATELY ELEVATED. NO. 8 IS AN ABERRANT AND UNCOMMON TYPE.

Photographs by Gifford and McKern

TONGAN TYPES SHOWING THE RANGE IN NOSE FORM, NOS. 1 TO 4 IN MEN AND NOS. 5 TO 8 IN WOMEN. NOS. 2, 3, 6, AND 7 ARE THE MOST COMMON FORMS. NONE OF THE NOSES HERE PORTRAYED APPROACHES IN SIZE THE CAUCASIAN TYPES.

Photographs by Gifford and McKern